C000007699

Jane McGuinness

Fashioning the New Woman

The Evolution of Women's Fashion During the Early Decades of 20th Century America

LAP LAMBERT Academic Publishing

Imprint

Any brand names and product names mentioned in this book are subject to trademark, brand or patent protection and are trademarks or registered trademarks of their respective holders. The use of brand names, product names, common names, trade names, product descriptions etc. even without a particular marking in this work is in no way to be construed to mean that such names may be regarded as unrestricted in respect of trademark and brand protection legislation and could thus be used by anyone.

Cover image: www.ingimage.com

Publisher:
LAP LAMBERT Academic Publishing
is a trademark of
International Book Market Service Ltd., member of OmniScriptum Publishing Group
17 Meldrum Street, Beau Bassin 71504, Mauritius

Printed at: see last page
ISBN: 978-3-659-92875-8

Copyright © Jane McGuinness
Copyright © 2019 International Book Market Service Ltd., member of OmniScriptum Publishing Group

The first three decades of the twentieth century saw a lot of change in America. This period, before, during and after the First World War, saw America emerge into a nation with industry, wealth and power in the new modern age. With this came a new American society in which an increasing number of people could afford time for leisure and extra money that could be spent on it. This emerging middle class was now able to spend their money on things that were previously only available to the very upper classes. Cars, vacations, and entertainment were suddenly available to the masses.

Nowhere can this change in society be seen more evidently, than in the fashion styles of the day. As was the case for much of what was previously considered a luxury, access to clothing that was considered fashionable began to trickle down into the middle classes. Where beforehand, a haute couture, French for high sewing, dress was the stuff of dreams for all but the very wealthiest of women, the growing wealth of the country and the middle class allowed for a larger populace interested in being fashionable. Suddenly, the majority of America was able to have clothing that was 'in style,' not only creating the need for the full blown American fashion industry that we have today, but also drastically changing the type of clothing that was widely worn. Through this drastic change in style and fashion taste, we can trace the development of the changing American society and our movement into the modern age, where fashion can be used for personal expression rather than personal confinement.

In this essay I will explore the dramatic change in fashion and popular style that occurred during this time. Through an examination of the cultural events and social changes of the pre-war, war, and post war eras, we will see a direct correlation between these changes and the major developments in the American fashion and the liberation of women from their clothing.

To understand the importance of the coming changes that women's fashion underwent during the second and third decades of the 20th century, we must first understand the basic rules that women's dress had followed for the previous several hundred years. Although there were many changes in style and silhouette that occurred in the time between the start of the Renaissance and the end of the Edwardian period, much of the structure of dresses, and especially the constricting undergarments that were suffered by women throughout this roughly four hundred year span, were constructed out of largely the same idea: that women's bodies could be molded and changed to fit the ideal body type and silhouette of the era.

These types of constrictions (figures 1,2) directly correlate with the woman's role in these respective societies. Take the Victorian era of fashion for example. The ideal shape of the female figure at the time Queen Victoria's reign began, in 1837, was very specific. It required a very thin waist line along with a very full 'ballet skirt'[1] and very full or puffy sleeves (figure 3). This shape, with slight alterations throughout the century, was largely consistent until the start of the Edwardian period around the turn of the century. The style was centered on the smallness of the waist.[2] There were several, very cumbersome, undergarments to help Victorian women achieve this harsh look by both physically taking the waist in as much as humanly possible, as well as using optical illusions such as full skirts to create the appearance of a smaller midsection.

----

[1] Alison Gernsheim, *Victorian and Edwardian Fashion: A Photographic Survey* (New York: Dover Publications, Inc., 1963), 27.

[2] Gernsheim, *Victorian and Edwardian Fashion*, 21.

Most important of these was the *stay* or the *corset*. "The aim of the stay was to create a smooth hard outline. It reduced a women's waist measurement by forcing it into a circular section, rather than a kidney shaped one, and accentuated the hips and breasts."[3] The stay is the perfect example of the constriction of women's fashion prior to the twentieth century. Corsets and stays were used for hundreds of years before the modern era but were changed slightly during each period to conform to the look that women were supposed to have during that time. A Victorian corset, (figure 4) emphasized the small waist whereas the Edwardian version (figure 5) focused on an S-curve silhouette,[4] creating the exaggerated curves that became popular around 1900.[5] The corset was by no means the only, and definitely not the worst, contraption that women had to suffer through prior to, and at the beginning of the twentieth century. *Gestation stays*, or pregnancy corsets, back straighteners, and tummy tuck devices,[6] just to name a few, were all part of any middle to upper class women's daily wardrobe.

Aspects of Victorian era clothing suggest what kind of lives women were expected to lead as well as reflect how they were thought of during the period. Diana Crane, in her book *Fashion and It's Social Agendas,* states: "Fashionable clothing exemplified the doctrine of separate spheres that was supported by other social institutions. It suited the subordinate and passive social roles women were expected to

---

[3] Sara Levitt, *Victorians Unbuttoned* (London: George Allen & Unwin Ltd, 1986), 26.

[4] Boucher, *20,000 Years of Fashion: The History of Costume and Personal Adornment* (New York: Harry N. Abrams, Inc.), 397.

[5] John Peacock, *Fashion Since 1900: The Complete Sourcebook* (London: Thames & Hudson Ltd., 1993), 9.

[6] Levitt, *Victorians Unbuttoned,* 29-30.

perform."[7] This ideal woman would have been modest, virtuous, and a good wife and mother. However attractive it was to be this ideal woman, it would have been a very restrictive life to lead. Women during this time were expected to live privately. The home was her domain, and although there were several acceptable public realms women could enter, they were still much suppressed in most aspects of their life and that included restriction by the clothing that was deemed appropriate for them.

These views on women and the construction of Victorian society were certainly not new in the nineteenth century. They had persisted for hundreds of years previous as did the continued effort of women's clothing to be restrictive and cumbersome. However, during the first few decades of the twentieth century, many things were changing societally, especially for women, that would rattle the long standing form. Among said changes were a growing middle class with more time for leisure, a waining religious influence on the population as a whole, and more of an open sexual expression among the forward thinking.[8] Along with these came several significant events such as the First World War, as well as women getting the right to vote in 1920. All of these, just to name a few, would become factors in the drastic reconstruction of women's clothing in the 1920's and the birth of modern fashion.

This change came relatively quickly, considering the slowness of the changes in style in the centuries previous. Starting slowly just before the Great War, it took a drastic turn in the years following. As we will addressed below, clothing had been slowly becoming more streamline, and less interested in a curvy figure, since the later half of

---

[7] Diana Crane, *Fashion and Its Social Agendas: Class, Gender, Identity in Clothing* (Chicago: The University of Chicago Press, 2000), 100.

[8] Paula S. Fass, *The Damned and the Beautiful: American Youth in the 1920's* (New York: Oxford 'niversity Press, 1977), 260.

the 1910's but by 1920 the voluptuous feminine form of the turn of the century was virtually gone, and replaced with a more boxy silhouette, showing very little waistline. Women also began to cut there hair very short during this period, contrasting the long hair done in intricate up-dos that was worn during the Edwardian period. By the mid 20's possibly the most major of these changes would come about: the shortening of the skirt's hemline, or length. This brought the length of the skirt to just bellow the knee and exposed the wearer's legs. This was the first time in the history of western women's popular fashion that the length of dress had risen more than an inch or two from the ground.[9]

In the following sections we will explore in more detail, these drastic changes that both fashion and society went through in the early decades of the twentieth century. Within this short period of time more progress and change happened in terms of fashion than had occurred in the several centuries previous put together, and just like during the Victorian era, women's clothing and fashion directly reflected the contemporary societal views of their time.

---

[9] Boucher, *20,000 Years of Fashion,* 400.

Advancement and Reform

At the start of the 1910's America was coming into it's own. The country's population was about 92 million and growing.[10] Immigrants were pouring into American cities at the rate of over a million per year, and the dominance of agricultural life was beginning to wane in favor of an urban lifestyle. Many of the concerns of Americans the decade before were changing as well. Modern inventions, medical and otherwise, were beginning to surface, making life more comfortable and stable for most in the country. [11] Things like the washing machine and the vacuum cleaner, for example, were just coming on the market around the start of the decade. This increasing stability would allow for growth in other ways, and it was in this decade that the United States became the World leader that it is today.[12]

At the start of the 1910's the ideal for women's beauty was a very specific type. This type: "tall and stately, superbly dressed, artful but never truly wicked,"[13] was called the Gibson Girl, and was created by Charles Dana Gibson, an illustrator for *Life* magazine in the 1890s. Although he seemingly never intended this for his drawings, they came to be considered, *the* American girl. A reporter for the New York *World* wrote: "Before Gibson synthesized his ideal woman, the American girl was vague, nondescript, and inchoate."[14] Women strove to be the Gibson Girl (figure 6) and men wanted to

---

[10] Ezra Bowen, ed., *1900-1910,* vol. 1 of *This Fabulous Century* (New York: Time-Life Books, 1969), 7.

[11] Ibid., 6.

[12] American Cultural History- The Twentieth Century, 1910-1920, Last modified November, 2011, http://kclibrary.lonestar.edu/decade10.html

[13] Bowen, *1900-1910,*183.

[14] Ibid.

marry her. Gibson drew her in serials, which ran in *Life* but she was also immortalized on all sorts of common and household items such as china plates, dresser sets, pillows, and even wall paper, which were marketed to young men as "just the thing for a bachelor apartment."[15] Her womanly and stately figure was what American girls were encouraged to look and dress like, but the Gibson girl would soon give way to a very different image of the ideal woman.

During this time Americans were beginning to enjoy more and more prosperity. and the gross domestic product kept rising. Benefits from industry and mass production were reaching more and more citizens, and life became, in some ways, easier. Passenger car sales were on the rise,[16] so people could travel and get around more easily. Houses were being outfitted with electricity. Electrication not only brought light into homes but also allowed for many more new appliances to make their way into daily life. Many of the appliances that, today, we consider common place, were just making their debut at the time.

For example, the first vacuum cleaner that was practical for home use was created in Ohio in 1907. It was developed for homes in the hopes that it would help those inflicted with asthma.[17] Also, the fist successful toaster was patented in 1909 by a Mr. Frank Shellor working for General Electric, a relatively new company at the time, having formed less than 20 years earlier, but one that goes on to dominates electric

---

[15] Ibid.

[16] Ezra Bowen, *1910-1920,* vol. 2 of *This Fabulous Century* (New York: Time-Life Books, 1969), 23.

[17] Greatest Achievements of the Twentieth Century, Household Appliance Timeline, Last modified 2014, http://www.greatachievements.org/?id=3768

innovations even today.[18] Another perfect example of the change in American's lives due to new technology come with the invention of the refrigerator. The first refrigerator was created for home use in 1913. This wasn't quite like the appliance we know today however. It was small, and was placed on top of an icebox or cold closet, and needed it's own plumbing source. Although the modern refrigerator would not be patented until 1929, the ability to control the temperature of food, therefore preserving it for much longer periods of time, greatly affected the way people bought and ate their food.[19]

For the most part, at first, these appliances would have been too pricey for most of middle class America, however, during the next ten years they would become more and more common place,[20]creating an easier and more comfortable lifestyle for those who benefited from them. An article in *Hearst's* magazine stated, just before the United States entered the First World War in 1917, that: "Never before was capital so plentiful. Never before were such profits rolled up by corporations. Never before were such wages enjoyed."[21] Why then, in this seemingly positive and prosperous time, when Americans were enjoying increasing convenience, was the country described as: "in a period of clamor, of bewilderment, of an almost tremulous unrest.... hastily reviewing all social conceptions... profoundly disenchanted"[22] by those in favor of social reformation?

---

[18] Ibid.

[19] Ibid.

[20] James C. Williams, *Technology and Engineering in the American Experience*, http://www.cr.nps.gov/history/resedu/bb_williams.htm

[21] *Hearst's* magazine, 1917, quoted in Ezra Bowen, *1910-1920*, vol. 2 of *This Fabulous Century* (New York: Time-Life Books, 1969), 23.

[22] Walter Weyl, *The New Democracy* (New York: The Micmillan Company, 1912) 1.

Despite American's new-found comfort, discontent grew during this pre-war period. Labor rights and women's suffrage, along with more radical causes such as the right to birth control or the call of a growing number of socialists for an overthrow of capitalism, were just a few of the demands that were beginning to be made on American society.[23] These attempts at social reform, combined with the growing wealth of the nation, helped to facilitate and shape a growing fashion industry and while all kinds of manufacturing were on the increase during this time, the fashion industry was able to combine both the growing prosperity, as well as the new social ideals, mainly concerning women, and ignite the beginnings of a drastic change in their clothing.

A major enabler of the change in fashion and the growing industry was the emergence of a new type of female: the "New Woman." Her main assertion was a woman's independence, as well as her equality with men. Some took a radical stance on this, such as Emma Goldman. Goldman was the leader of a group of new women who were active in the Greenwich Village area of New York City, which, even then, was a mecca for those who chose a bohemian lifestyle, attracting artists and racialists alike.[24] Goldman and her comrades were particularly emancipated and anarchist, even for the new women. They advocated the ideal of 'free love' and their right to as liberated and unquestioned a sex life as men had. She gave lectures on this double standard which forced women into a chastity that was not expected of men.[25] Not all new women were as radical as those coming out of Greenwich Village however, some were just

---

[23] 'Bowen, *1910-1920*, 23.

[24] The Greenwich Village Society for Historic Preservation, Bohemia,1900-1929, last modified 2014, http://www.gvshp.org/_gvshp/resources/history.htm

[25] Bowen, *1910-1920,* 30.

focused on what could be considered the primary objective of those of the women who were, even slightly, politically active: their right to vote.

The right to vote defined feminism in the 1910's. Before this decade there had been some progress in the suffrage movement, but it was on much smaller scales. Women such as Susan B. Anthony and Lucretia Coffin Mott had succeeded in obtaining the vote for women in several states, but the large majority of American woman were still denied the right that the whole country, excepting criminals, lunatics and, of course, women, had access to.[26]

This crawling progress was amped up starting in 1910 as the growing number of determined women of the decade set out to create change for themselves and generations of women to come. Unlike what the fight for women's right to vote had been like in the previous decades, the freedom of this era, especially concerning women, contributed to a change in the way the majority of women felt about the rights. Whereas before, a select few had fought for the cause, leaving the majority, seemingly unconcerned with suffrage, at home, 1910 started an era were women's rights and suffrage were finally acceptable, and even fashionable things to advocate for amongst the new, more liberated, women of America,[27] unlike their mothers and grandmothers. As a suffragist, whose mother and then husband had discouraged her marching in New York's suffrage parades, stated: "my girlhood Mother had repeated that a lady should

---

[26] Ibid., 42.

[27] Ibid.

never allow herself to be conspicuous. To march up Fifth Avenue had promised to flout

directly one's early training."[28]

This woman's generation decided that they did not care about what their

predecessors considered unladylike. She goes on to state, in her description of the

parade she eventually overcame her family to attend, that: "When it's done along with

twenty-five thousand other women, nothing could seem more natural. Embarrassment is

left at the street corner, and one is just a part, a singing, swinging part of a great stream,

all flowing in the same direction toward the same goal."[29] As the decade continued,

more and more women, and men as well, such as the Men's League for Women's

Suffrage,[30] joined the cause. The parades grew, some numbering in the 40,000s. As the

suffragette demonstrates in her article, these women were not their mothers.

Regardless of their level of emancipation, these women were described as

"independent, bright-eyed, alert, [and] alive"[31] by those who observed them, and

although there were some men, and certainly older women, who did not approve of the

New Woman's behavior, many were enchanted by her. H.L. Mencken, editor of the

magazine *Smart Set,* describes the New Woman:

Her skirts have just reached her very trim and pretty ankles; her hair, coiled upon

her skull, has just exposed the ravishing whiteness of her neck. A charming

---

[28] *The Outlook* magazine, 1915, quoted in Ezra Bowen, *1910-1920,* vol. 2 of *This Fabulous Century* (New York: Time-Life Books, 1969), 46.

[29] Ibid.

[30] Bowen, *1910-1920,* 46.

[31] *The Ladies Home Journal,* quoted in Ezra Bowen, *1910-1920,* vol. 2 of *This Fabulous Century* (New York: Time-Life Books, 1969), 30.

creature! There is something trim and trig and confident about her. She is easy in her manners. There is music in her laugh. She is youth, she is hope, she is romance - she is wisdom!"[32]

And as Mencken briefly describes, along with this New Woman, came a new way of dress that fit her liberated personality (figure 7).

The New Woman was *doing* more than the women of the previous generations. At the start of the second decade there were roughly 7.5 million woman in the workforce. This number would jump to about 8.5 million by 1920.[33] Even when not in work, woman seemed to be more mobile than their more domesticated and stagnant mothers and grandmothers. Women could be seen out and about, driving cars or taking trollies or subways, at the movies or taking lunch breaks. These more worldly women refused to suffer the previously constricting styles that were worn by Victorian women, who sat in their parlors and remained at home all day. The mobility of the New Woman required her to actually be able to move in what she was wearing. "When the emancipated woman slid into the new styles of the decade, it was obvious to the admiring males she was freeing herself of more than social restraints. Gone was the tight corset that had pinched in her waist until she could barely breathe. Now, if her figure tended to spread out, then so be it."[34] The beginnings of change during this

---

[32] H.L Mencken, *Smart Set* magazine, quoted in Ezra Bowen, *1910-1920,* vol. 2 of *This Fabulous Century* (New York: Time-Life Books, 1969), 36.

[33] Bowen, *1910-1920,* 34.

[34] Ibid., 36.

period, although slight at first, were growing side by side with the slowly expanding

freedom that the New Woman was fighting for.

Although the hemline of skirts had risen to ankle length by 1910,[35] the length of

skirts continued to rise slowly throughout the decade. By 1915 a women's skirt would

reveal the bottom of her calves, showing either boots or shoes with stockings that would

be worn to cover up a woman's legs.[36] In addition to this, necklines were, ever so

slightly, moving lower, exposing a little bit of the collar bone and chest (figure 8).

Although these alterations hardly seem scandalous to us now, it is clear that these were

considered radical by conservatives of the day. Even as early as 1913, a clergyman

states: "Never in history were the modes so abhorrently indecent as they are today."[37]

Along with a slight but increasing exposure of skin, however, women's clothing

also took a turn for the looser. As corsets were becoming less and less popular, clothing

became less focused on a cinched waist, and therefore a curvy figure. Starting even at

the beginning of the decade, this trend continued to become more and more obvious

and by 1915 clothing was not at all formfitting, with women wearing dresses that hung

from them with very little shape aside from a loose belt (figure 9). This looser, straighter

style allowed women more flexibility. Although corsets were still in use,[38] they were not

necessary to provide this new silhouette because a woman's waist and traditional

'hourglass figure' were not emphasized quite as much. This provided the increased

---

[35] Peacock, *Fashion Since 1900,* 36.

[36] Ibid., 44.

[37] Bowen, *1910-1920,* 37.

[38] Peacock, *Fashion Since 1900,* 42.

flexibility in women's lifestyle that fit the concept of the New Woman. As she was liberated and unrestricted, so should her clothing be.

Thus, as fashionable people were become more interested in the ability to pursue a broader range of activities, fashion was becoming more utilizable. In an issue of *Vogue* magazine, in January 1913, an article was written about a change in New York's society women. It seems these women, who previously had the reputation of only caring to "dine and dance and gossip"[39] had taken an interest in the intellectual and art scene at the time. Although it is stated that this union of interests had failed before, it was successful in 1913. Previously "the fashionables were wont to patronize the 'geniuses,' and they would not be dragged to [their] entertainments... because these assemblages were not 'smart.'"[40] In return "The writers and artists... were too much occupied with their own more serious interests to understand frivolities."[41] These two differing groups did, however, manage to come together at this time and form what the author, Walter G. Robinson, calls "a Salon of Wit and Fashion."[42] Robinson attributes this union with boredom. However it came about, though, this development shows the inclination for fashionable women towards more grounded interests. This was high society's version of a New Women, and although these women certainly still did not work, and definitely still dined and gossiped, they also turned their attention to a social group that was much more liberated and independent than their own.

---

[39] Walter G. Robinson, *Vogue,* Jan 1913, pictured in Nathalie Herschdorfer, *Coming into Fashion: A Century of Photography at Conde Nast* (New York: Prestel Publishing, 2012), 27.

[40] Ibid.

[41] Ibid.

[42] Ibid.

This example from the upper classes of New York society demonstrates an overarching change in the attitudes of women. The New Woman was slowly taking over the Gibson Girl and the previous American Ideal. The picture that accompanies Robinson's article is a painting of a Mrs. Benjamin Guinness, a New York Socialite, in a loose fitting coat, with a fur lined collar, a cropped hair cut, and small bowl hat. The caption reads: "one of the cleverest New York Society Women, initiated the new social movement."[43] It is significant that the New Woman was strongly represented on two fronts. She was not only the average middle class woman that was seen on a day to day basis but she was also represented in the pages of magazines and in newspapers. These were the women who influenced the haute couture in the fashion industry, and thus, enabled the complete transformation of the current style.

With the social reforms affecting most of American society, there was not much, excepting the most conservative, who were a growing minority, in the way of the increasing independence of women and therefore, the drastic changes to what women were choosing to wear. Both fashion and societal changes were on the rise and, although they may have continued in these developments, the United States' declaration of War in the spring of 1917, and America's sudden thrust into a wartime mentality would accelerate these sorts of changes.

---

[43] Ibid.

The Great War and America

World War One broke out in Europe on the 28th of July, 1914. However, during the war's first few years the United States remained officially neutral while supplying large amounts of aid to Britain and France. In April of 1917 President Woodrow Wilson officially issued a declaration of war against Germany. Before entering the war, the U.S. military was relatively weak. But as the war in Europe and the war efforts at home progressed, America, along with the U.S. military, grew stronger. America emerged from the war, both economically and militarily, the most powerful country in the World.[44] The 'splendid struggle,"[45] as the war on the home front has been describes, fostered a unique collaborative effort amongst American people that resulted in their catapult into the modern age. Where changes and reforms were slowly making progress in the earlier part of the decade, the Great War sped them up, and launched changes in woman's fashion, amongst most other aspects of American culture already in transition into modernity.

The pre-war U.S. Army contained exactly 208,034 men, with the air service, amounting to 55 planes and 130 pilots.[46] American's had also not fought in a major war since the Civil War, which had ended over 52 years before the U.S. entered WWI. A lack of military experience and capable man power made the war effort tough at first. The

---

[44] Bowen, *1910-1920,* 208.

[45] Ibid.

[46] Ibid.

draft was implemented in June of 1917, which yielded almost 10 million men through volunteering alone.[47] Although this quickly solved the problem of numbers, it came with issues of its own. Because this was largely a civilian army, most of the volunteers being farmers and country boys, there was little to no combat experience among them. There was also a shortage of equipment. Theodor Roosevelt wrote, while in the training camps, that: "the enormous majority of our men in the encampments were drilling with broomsticks or else with rudely whittled guns.... In the camps I saw barrels mounted on sticks on which zealous captains were endeavoring to teach their men how to ride a horse."[48] With most of their military supplies being purchased from the British and French governments during that first year of American involvement, it was necessary for the country to rally to its forces aid in order to fulfill President Wilson's goal, that: "The world must be made safe for democracy."[49]

There were many ways that the American public was able to provide for their soldiers at war. One of the most obviously important ones was through financial support. A major way that this was accomplished was through the sale of Liberty bonds. These allowed American's to purchase a bond, or many, for a small price, in which they would receive between a 3.5 to a 4.25 percent interest rate when they went to reclaimed them after the war.[50] There was a great push to get American's to subscribe to these bonds. Celebrities would perform skits and entice their audiences to buy bonds. Bond peddlers

---

[47] Ibid., 211.

[48] Theodore Roosevelt, quoted in Ezra Bowen, *1910-1920,* vol. 2 of *This Fabulous Century* (New York: Time-Life Books, 1969), 208.

[49] President Woodrow Wilson, quoted in Ezra Bowen, *1910-1920,* vol. 2 of *This Fabulous Century* (New York: Time-Life Books, 1969), 208.

[50] Museum of American Finance, Libery Bond, last modified 2014, http://www.moaf.org/exhibits/checks_balances/woodrow-wilson/liberty-bond

would go across country selling them, and President Wilson was known to make personal appeals, once even showing up at a Broadway play to attempt to enlist subscribers.[51] All of these efforts worked and by the end of the war Americans had raised $17 billion from bonds alone. With the U.S. population being about 100 million at the time, each person, on average, could boast of raising about $170 to aid their country. The Liberty bond system not only allowed the war to be waged across the Atlantic, but it also greatly benefited the people at home. Many Americans who, before, had not had the ability to save much money, were able to collect considerable sums from their bonds after they were eligible. This was a contributing factor in the increasing wealth of the American middle class during the decade of the 20's.

Money, however, was not the only thing that was needed for the continued war effort. The U.S. government, led by Herbert Hoover and the Food Administration, was also advocating the conservation of food and other commonly used products in order for the troops overseas to benefit from them. Citizens were urged to plant backyard gardens in order to grow their own food. They were also encouraged to observe days such as 'wheatless' Mondays and Wednesdays, 'meatless' Tuesdays and 'porkless' Thursdays. Unlike the efforts during World War Two, participation in rationing was voluntary but many Americans were dedicated to it, some even going so far as to attach horses to the front of their cars so they could better observe 'gasless' Sundays, another implemented ration.[52]

---

[51] Bowen, *1910-1920*, 215.

[52] Ibid., 222.

The people at home contributed in other small ways as well. Word was getting back about the conditions in the trenches, which led the American Red Cross to issue appeals for knitted goods, such as socks and sweaters for the soldiers. Pictures can be seen of groups of young boys knitting away, seemingly pleased with their contribution. Families at home also endeavored to save peach pits, as they could be used in the making of gas masks to aid against the threat of mustard gas and other chemical weapons that were a danger to men in the trenches. Even household items, such as books to give the troops some reading material, were donated in large quantities to help with the effort.[53] While some of these books were probably not the most suitable for men at war,[54] and there is some speculation as to whether the knitted goods ever actually reached soldiers in the trenches,[55] it was never the less the endeavor of the American citizens to do anything they possibly could to play their small part in the Great War.

For many women, however, playing their part meant much more than donating books and rationing their food. With most of the American work force being men, after the start of the war, the country was largely depleted of workers. Not only were workers needed for general jobs which needed to be carried on, there was also a great urgency for artillery, war machines and other goods, to be manufactured. With most of the working men gone overseas, it was up to the women to take over this role:

---

[53] Ibid., 228.

[54] *The Literary Digest*, 1918, quoted in Ezra Bowen, *1910-1920*, vol. 2 of *This Fabulous Century* (New York: Time-Life Books, 1969), 231.

[55] Samuel Dale, *Chronicle* magazine, quoted in Ezra Bowen, *1910-1920*, vol. 2 of *This Fabulous Century* (New York: Time-Life Books, 1969), 228.

America was confronted with the spectacle of women auto mechanics,

telegraph messengers, elevator operators and streetcar conductors - and that

was not all. They toiled on factory assembly lines, carried ice, plowed fields and

became traffic cops. Women invaded even the sanctuary of the armed forces,

about 11,000 female yeomen enlisted in the Navy as clerks and stenographers.[56]

Though some people, such as the Committee for the Protection of Girls,[57] thought this

was a detriment to young women, on a whole America embraced this and the working

women relished their new tasks and their ability to be part of the cause. A journalist for

The Independent magazine, Norma B. Kastl, took to interviewing some of these women.

She found that even people of some fame, such as musicians, stage actresses, and

artist were taking up work, stating: "One well-known portrait painter is now spending her

days in turning over little brass disks and carefully inspecting both sides."[58] One woman

that she interviewed, who had previously created a few famous characters in Broadway

plays, describes her feelings about working in a factory in New York City:

I would not have missed it for anything. It has been one the richest experiences

of my live - meeting all the wonderful women who are there, not only the

professional women but the little seamstresses and factory girls who have given

[56] Bowen, *1910-1920*, 219.

[57] Ibid.

[58] Norma B. Kastl, *The Independent* magazine, quoted in Ezra Bowen, *1910-1920*, vol. 2 of *This Fabulous Century* (New York: Time-Life Books, 1969), 220.

up their old work to do their bit - and all the time feeling that I was being really useful to the boys on the other side.[59]

All American people, and especially these women, underwent a drastic lifestyle change during those few war years. This change in values and priorities, even for this short period of time, had profound effects on American society as a whole. One notable affect was that the efforts of the working woman to support the war also greatly aided their fight for women's suffrage.

One slogan that was used by some female workers during the war period was: "Equal Pay for Equal Work,"[60] which asserted their right to the same wage the men had been paid for that same job before the war. This idea goes hand in hand with their cry for the vote and much of their argument for suffrage was reinforced by their demonstrated ability to work any job that a man once did. This further emphasized an equality of genders and created a bigger drive within the female community. More and more women began to feel that if they could work and do jobs just as men do, then they should be able to vote like men as well. This recruited many more women to the suffrage cause and helped push the issue to the forefront of people's minds. Whereas before the war, all that would have been seen of the suffragist's attempts at reform were the parades and demonstrations, which were mainly concentrated in larger cities, during the war people saw women working and earning a man's salary. This was a subtle but effective way of stating that they should be equal.

----

[59] Ibid.

[60] Bowen, *1910-1920*, 220.

The changes in women's attitudes accompanying their general lifestyle created changes in what they were choosing to wear as well. There was a conservativeness about the clothing during these war years. As stated in the first section, the styles of this decade became increasingly loose and less cumbersome. This trend continues on during the war, where skirts become noticeably wider at the bottom and falling just above the ankle. This allowed working women, especially those who were serving as nurses or members of the Navy a freedom of mobility.[61] The lack of a prominent waistline and the strait silhouette of this style diminished any feminine curves and created a less curvy, more masculine shape. Alison Lurie, author of *The Language of Clothes,* describes this look: "Thousands of women entered the second decade of the century shaped like hour glasses and came out of it shaped like rolls of carpet."[62]

During the First World War, women's fashion also started to adopt the look of the military uniforms being worn by the soldiers. Lauren Topor, in her article: "War and Fashion: Political Views and How Military Styles Influence Fashion," argues that this trend in WWI is the beginning of a reoccurring style that has appeared during many American wars since.[63] The military uniforms of this war were tailored to men flighting in the trenches. This meant several things in terms of their garments. The men's clothing were camouflaged and blended in with the dirt and mud of the trenches. The uniforms were also made from wool and were thick and durable. These outfits were decorated

---

[61] Allison Lurie, *The Language of Clothes* (New York: Random House, 1983), 73.

[62] Ibid.

[63] Lauren Topor, "War and Fashion: Political Views and How Military Styles Influence Fashion" (2008). Master's Theses and Doctoral Dissertations. Paper 168., 1.

with metal badges that displayed the persons rank. This is also when the zipper emerges as a fastening agent.[64]

As Topor argues, these styles made their way into the clothing of the civilians at home. An army style jacket came into popularity (figure 10). These were worn looser, as mentioned above, and widened at the hips. They were decorated with wide belts and large side pockets.[65] The colors of civilian style also took from the military uniform. Browns, dark grays and Khakis were the common hues and the fabrics were frequently made from wool and other substantial and tough materials.[66] The use of epaulettes, which were prominent in the uniforms of high ranking officers and on the ceremonial uniforms made it's way into women's fashion as well. Another major development in fashion that came from the World War One military uniform, and is still popular today, is the trench coat (figure 11). This is a version of the overcoat that was worn by soldiers in the trenches, hence the name, and was meant to protect against the elements,[67] a function that it still serves on both men and women today. This militarization of women's clothing contributed to the masculinity that their styles were portraying.

To add to this change in clothing frame and inspiration, women were also adopting a shorter, cropped hair style, 'the bob.' This cut, although worn by some forward thinkers beforehand, largely got its start during the war years.[68] Long hair, which

---

[64] Ibid., 2.

[65] Ibid.

[66] Ibid.

[67] Ibid.

[68] Peacock, *Fashion Since 1900*, 45.

had been traditionally worn by western women for most of history,[69] became

cumbersome and ill-suited for the work that many women were doing during this time.

This could perhaps be seen as a slightly stronger, tougher look that was used to assert

the woman's ability to be like a man, and do men's work. Although this style was coming

into fashion before the war, the still lessening prominence of a waistline was completed

during those years,[70] and the transformation into masculine figures was better realized

(figure 12). This further asserted the women's belief that they were equal with men.

Aside from the changes in fashionable clothing during the period of war, for many

women, a shift towards more practical garments became necessary. Women who had

taken up the jobs that men left behind, at least for their work day, had to reject what was

in vogue all together, in favor of clothing that was more suited to a life of labour (figure

13). These are some of the first images of women in significant number wearing pants,

and the idea of pants for women, although not become widespread for several decades,

does gain steady popularity among more radical females during and after these war

years, especially in leisure wear.[71]

Although there were significant changes in inspiration being drawn into the

fashionable mix during the war, the changes to the overall silhouette in war time were

relatively slight. The results of World War One, which was ended in November of 1918,

in which the Allied forces prevailed, establishing the United States as the most powerful

country in the world, caused a much more drastic change than the war itself had.

American society had adopted to accommodate for the war efforts, and in the post war

---

[69] Ibid.

[70] Peacock, *Fashion Since 1900,* 46.

[71] Ibid., 67.

years they would change again, this time for the more extravagant, liberated, and radical. Fashion, too, took this giant leap into the modern age, as they referred to it.[72] Women's clothing would, for the first time, take a drastic step in a different direction than it had been going for hundreds of year. It is in this post war decade that the way we address the clothing that we wear, and how we choose to present ourselves, was born and clothing became a way in which women could express their individuality.

---

[72] Alison Lurie, *The Language of Clothes* (New York: Random House, 1983), 73.

The Roaring 20's

The 1920's has been described as a strictly cultural decade.[73] It's situation between two major political events, World War One and the Great Depression, along with the fact that the decade boasts minimal political or reform activities, makes it hard to consider the 20's in either of those lights. What the decade did have, however, was a new and unique culture, rejecting that of the more sober generation before. The 20's replaced the seriousness and grown-up ideals of the previous two decades with a mood of escapism on the part of both the people and the government. If the world had problems, American's just chose to ignore them on a large scale. The decade was reflected in a common toast from the period: "Eat, drink and be merry, for tomorrow we die."[74] This suggests an age of youth and independence, but also, of pessimism, and a willful ignorance of reality.[75]

This change in attitudes of the people can be seen in the personalities of the two presidents that represent them. Woodrow Wilson, the man who led America through the War, and brought the country to their position of world leadership, was a scholarly man. He was an idealist, and focused on reform and the responsibilities of the U.S.[76] However, by the 1920's, the time of reform and activism was in the past. President Warren Harding, Wilson's successor was a very different sort of leader. He is described as being light hearted and humorous as well as somewhat childlike, not unlike the public

---

[73] Fass, *The Damned and the Beautiful*, 4.

[74] Ezra Bowen, ed., *1920-1930*, vol. 1 of *This Fabulous Century* (New York: Time-Life Books, 1969), 26.

[75] Ibid., 24.

[76] Ibid., 23.

at the time. He may not have been the most competent of presidents-- most of his friends and 'cronies' were involved in one scandal or another-- but he embodied the peoples' ideals at the time and managed to continue in popularity despite these shortcomings.[77] Harding died suddenly in August, 1923, and was succeeded by Calvin Coolidge, who continued Harding's policies and ideals. Known for his relaxed demeanor, and being famous for taking at least a two hour nap every work day, Coolidge embodied the child without responsibilities.[78]

It is important to note, however, that the general idea we have of the twenties, wasn't the case for all of America. Many of the people in rural areas of the country new little to nothing of what was happening in the larger cities, only experiencing 'the roaring 20's' through the films that more and more Americans were enjoying on a weekly basis.[79] Out of this lingering conservatism comes a phenomenon that is unique to the 1920's but seems to be counterintuitive considering the exploits of the time period. This movement was prohibition.

The war of 'Wet' versus 'Dry,' as it has been called by some historians,[80] could be seen as a remnant from the previous, idealistic and reformist America of the decade before. The prohibitionist's stance was that they were not against the working class drinker. They believed that it was a system of injustice that had made him like that, and were attempting to rewrite that system. They were not opposing the man who drinks but rather the reason which forced him into doing so. This rejection of a societal construct

---

[77] Ibid., 24.

[78] Ibid.

[79] Ibid., 25.

[80] Paul Carter, *The Twenties in America* (New York: Thomas Y. Crowell Company, 1968), 69.

that they believed unjust is characteristic of the 1910's and it's many social reforms
addressed above. This idealistic idea doesn't quite fit into the new ideals of the 20's,
however, it becomes the central controversy of the time. As Historian Clarke Chambers
notes, "Prohibition was a divisive issue, particularly for the professional settlement
workers and caseworkers who were increasingly torn between their sure knowledge that
alcohol so often meant unhappiness for their neighbors and clients, and their
commitment to personal liberty."[81]

Prohibition was put into law at almost the exact opening of the decade, framing
the 20's as this singular time and making liquor, beer and wine illegal throughout the
country. However well-meaning the intent of the amendment, the majority of the nation
did not take prohibition seriously; it is speculated that never in the history of the U.S.
has a law been so 'flagrantly violated.'[82] Not only did Americans largely not abide by this
law, but it was most likely responsible for an increase in alcohol consumption and
exacerbated the county's drinking problem. People not only, drank more, but often more
people drank. Women, for example, who were previously not allowed into bars or
saloons, began to frequent the speakeasies, or underground bars and clubs, that were
where people would gather to drink out of the sight of the law.[83]

Along with the increased number of law breakers, just from those who continued
to drink, prohibition also elevated crime levels in other ways. Smuggling and
bootlegging, for example, became very popular during this period. Ships loaded with

[81] Clarke Chambers, quoted in Paul Carter, The Twenties in America (New York: Thomas Y. Crowell
Company, 1968), 69.

[82] Bowen, 1920-1930, 154.

[83] Ibid.

alcohol would be waiting off the coasts and anyone with access to a rowboat could easily acquire all the alcohol they desired.[84] Bootleggers would make their own alcohol to sell for an elevated price. Some would also go so far as to steel from the warehouses full of government consigned alcohol that had been manufactured just before the law was enacted.[85] There was also an evident rise in organized crime due to prohibition. Mobsters saw the selling of liquor as a lucrative business opportunity, and it was these groups that frequently ran the speakeasies that American's were flocking to.[86]

Along with these problems, prohibition also faced the issue of enforcement. The police officers didn't necessarily agree with the law that they were supposed to be enforcing and this created problems. Many officers would take bribes for their discretion and then go ahead and join the drinkers at the speakeasies. Fiorello H. La Guardia, a congressman at the time and the future mayor of New York City, stated that it would take 250,000 men to enforce the law in the city, however it would take another 200,000 men to police the police."[87] Other jobs charged with the task of controlling the 'wets,' such as the Prohibition Bureau, had the highest turnover rates out of any government agency and were described as "a training school for bootleggers."[88]

Citizens, with the help from these less-than-committed law enforcers, got creative with their ways to conceal their drinking habits. Flasks became a must-have item, and conveniently baggy clothing covered up any bulges created by tins or pouches of

---

[84] Ibid.

[85] Ibid., 170.

[86] Ibid., 154.

[87] Fiorrello H. La Guardia, quoted in Ezra Bowen, ed., *1920-1930,* vol. 1 of *This Fabulous Century* (New York: Time-Life Books, 1969), 154.

[88] Bowen, *1920-1930,* 159.

alcohol (figure 14). There are accounts of people going so far as to drain eggs and refill them with liquor to smuggle them into the country,[89] and both woman and men were known to carry around hollow canes, filled with alcohol, that they could simply unplug and add to any drink. Considering it's unpopularity, it's not surprising that prohibition, in the end did not win out, and eventually, was repealed in 1933. Unfortunately for the prohibitionists, the split that it cause within the nation, and the backlash that it received from those who opposed it probably created more problems than it solved, and in many ways, fostered the society that was born out of it: "The roaring 20's."

With the combination of the underground social scenes and the disobedience towards the law, along with the culture of youth already established, came an atmosphere of party and extravagance. Out of this came a major music phenomenon: The Jazz Age. This new kind of music, and the dances that went with it were, once again, embraced by the youth of the nation. The older generations were not necessarily as enthused. An upstate New York preacher stated that: "Jazz may be analyzed as a combination of nervousness, lawlessness, primitive and savage animalism and lasciviousness."[90] Much to their dismay, however, the Jazz movement caught on like wildfire.

Jazz had originated from New Orleans and moved up river, eventually to Chicago, and then over to New York. Even with it's increasing popularity, it remanded largely concentrated within the African American communities such as Harlem and the South Side of Chicago.[91] The white population's fascination with the jazz culture steadily

---

[89] Ibid.

[90] Ibid., 76.

[91] Ibid.

grew though, and it eventually made leaps to the 'mainstream,' including several Negro Broadway plays[92] centered around jazz and many successful records. However some would claim that these most successful Jazz musicians, such as Paul Whiteman, were not playing real jazz at all, while the real artists, like Louis Armstrong, were struggling to make a buck.[93]

Another large part of the reason that the 20's had such an over-the-top atmosphere was that, the U.S. was experiencing a huge economic boom. There had been a two year recession immediately following the war, however, by the early years of the decade, business was booming.[94] President Coolidge described this American obsession with making money: "The business of America is business."[95] This surge in business was across the board, affecting not just banking and stocks, but the entirety of the economy.[96]

One of these sectors was the printed word, and Americans began to crave newspaper and magazine coverage more than ever. From the *New York Times,* where they could get their foreign correspondence, to high profile exposés, which were the make of every good paper, to the less the respectable, tabloid magazines, that told gossip or the 'titillating' stories told in the magazines such as *True Story,*[97] American's couldn't get enough of the printed word.

---

[92] Ibid., 89.

[93] Ibid., 76.

[94] Ibid., 96.

[95] Calvin Coolidge, quoted in Ezra Bowen, ed., *1920-1930,* vol. 1 of *This Fabulous Century* (New York: Time-Life Books, 1969), 96.

[96] Bowen, *1920-1930,* 96.

[97] Ibid., 180.

This obsession with newspapers and magazines fostered another sector in American business: Advertisement. The advertising industry had been growing steadily since the 1880, using extra newspaper space, and creating catalogues such as Sears Roebuck or for department stores such as Macy's,[98] but the by 1920 the growth of the total advertising volume in the United States had reached $3 billion, and continued to increase throughout the decade.[99] With the business boom, there was extra money to spend, and consumerism became the way of American life. American citizen's desire to purchase, along with the increased interest in print, created a perfect opportunity for advertisement to capitalize. While people got their daily gossip or news fix, they could also get their consumer one. American ads attempted to sell everything from cars and appliances, to clothing (figure 15), and the Fashion industry experienced a huge growth because of this.

It is possible that this advertising craze aided in the creation of 'fashion photography' as a genre of art. Photographer and artist Edward Steinchen came to America to work as chief photographer at Condé Nast Publications, the publishers of Vogue, in 1923. Previously working for french magazines, he brought the ideas of fashion photography to the United States. Disliking the 'pictorialist' and plain pictures that had ruled fashion images, his approach was to create art out of his models and the adds they were producing. His idea of what successful fashion photography is, was that it should embody "distinction, elegance and chic."[100] This new style of photography and

---

[98] American Advertising: A brief History, last modified April 17, 2014, http://historymatters.gmu.edu/mse/ads/amadv.html

[99] Ibid.

[100] Nathalie Herschdorfer, *Coming into Fashion: A Century of Photography at Conde Nast* (New York: Prestel Publishing, 2012), 32.

advertising, that "conjured an image of luxury and seduction,"[101] contributed to fashion's ability to grow though advertisement.

The emphasis on the youth culture, mentioned above, spanned all aspects of daily life for the people that embraced it. So, naturally, fashion adopted this ideal and transformed to help its wearers proclaim their youth. As addressed in the two previous sections, trends towards change had begun as early as 1910, however, during the post war period in America, these changes developed rapidly, and in a matter of a few years, fashion was so drastically different that it is hard to believe that only a decade or so had gone by.[102]

In the quest to be childlike, fashion styles drew directly from the styles worn by children since the turn of the century. These smocks, or sac like dresses would have been almost exactly what the women wearing them would have worn in their childhood. The slightly masculine and tough look of the war years was out, and this look grew younger, along with the American mentality, transforming into that of a boy or prepubescent girl.[103] Skirts continued to rise until they reached a plateau, around 1925, and remained at a level just bellow the knee until 1929 (figure 16).[104] Waist lines, as well, continued on their loosening trend discussed before, and after 1920, were virtually gone altogether. Women would either wear their dress as a strait sheath or it would be

---

[101] Ibid.

[102] Lurie, *The Language of Clothes*, 73.

[103] Ibid.

[104] Peacock, *Fashion Since 1900*, 69.

loosely belted at hip level (figure 17).[105] This emerging look, and the women that went along with it, was called the 'flapper:'

> Though she might have the figure of an adolescent boy, her face was that of a small child: round and soft, with a turned-up nose, saucer eyes and a pouting "bee-stung" mouth. Her bobbed hair curled about her head like a child's, or clung to it like a babies.[106] (figure 18)

Fashion contributed to the flapper look in many ways. Not only were the styles of the day inspired by those that had been worn in childhood, but the fabrics were as well. The tough and durable fabrics of the war years were replaced with soft, fine material, and were usually lighter in color. Cream, soft pastels, and white colors that young girls would wear, were widely used in adult dressmaking during this period. Along with the silhouette and fabric choices, the proportions also contributed to the look of youth.[107] The clothing often had the appearance of being too big for women, and made them look, comparatively, small and childlike.

Accessories, during this period, also contributed to the youthfulness of the flapper women. The hat that is associated with the 1920's is called the cloche. These emerged about half way through the decade and were "adopted as uniform."[108] By the end of the decade they were a completely brimless hat that fit tightly on the head (figure

---

[105] Ibid., 61.

[106] Lurie, *The Language of Clothes*, 74.

[107] Ibid., 75.

[108] Fiona Clark, *Hats: The Costume Accessories Series* (London: Anchor Brendon Ltd., 1982), 52.

19). A modified version of the 'Mary Jane' shoes that young girls would have worn (figure 20) were adopted as well. A heal was added for women and they became the common, every day shoe for the era.[109] Even with this growth of informality in the shortening of dresses, and showing of skin, women were still expected to wear gloves when going out. This understood rule, the same went for hats, did not really go out of fashion until the 1960's, however, as seen with the hats, they became as minimalistic as possible, almost as if they weren't being worn.[110]

All the aspects of the changing fashion can be traced back to youthfulness. The American mentality at the time went through an enormous alteration itself. To reject the maturity of their parents and avoid the responsibilities that they deemed to much of a burden, they chose to revert to the time of their youth, where there were no responsibilities and only play. Fashion, as it has done before, followed and adapted to this mentality, allowing women to express this new freedom from pressures and responsibility while framing them in their youth.

---

[109] Lurie, *The Language of Fashion,* 74.

[110] Valerie Cumming, *Gloves: The Costume Accessories Series* (London: Anchor Brendon Ltd., 1982), 76.

Conclusions

As fashions and styles continued to evolve throughout the following decades, an overall trend can be seen in the increasing inclination towards comfort and utility. There was a not so steady development in the trend towards comfort. Periods such as the 1950's, where a more restrictive, although still less concealing look, known as the 'new look,' ironically, was back in style. However, this was quickly eclipsed by the trends of the 1960's, in which miniskirts made their entrance into fashion and women could wear pants without scrutiny.

Since this time, American fashion could be what the individual woman wants it to be. If she upholds comfort above all, she can wear sweatpants or leggings. If being uncomfortable doesn't bother her so much, she can dress herself in pencil skirts and stilettos. Today, style is about personal expression. Our ability to do this wouldn't be the same if it weren't for the drastic changes in fashion, as well as American society that developed during the twenty year period between 1910-1930.

For Americans, this time was full of change and evolution. People went from a time a hard work and labour, to a time of convenience and prosperity. Women went from a time of oppression and stagnancy to a time of independence and mobility, and a time when they could express their opinions and vote for themselves. The mentality of Americans also changed. They went from the desire to reform and better their circumstances to the desire to forget about the problems of the world and reject the seriousness they felt weighed down by.

Throughout all these changes, we can trace the development that fashion underwent as well. While American women focused on suffrage and reform, the clothing that they wore reflected this in it's loosening and flowing freedom that embodied the new women's liberation as well. During the conservative war years, fashion took on a masculine and military look, echoing the working women, showing their equality to men as well as their support for their troops. And finally, after women had their vote, and when the worlds problem became too cumbersome for the American people to address and they reverted back to a childlike naïvety and freedom, fashion did as well, dressing women in what they wore when they were children and freeing them from the conservative, rigid, and constricting styles that had been worn by women from hundreds of years.

This freedom sparked a trend in fashion that, in some ways, continues today. Never again have women gone back to a style where everyday dresses are floor length, and although some might have chosen to wear corsets during a few periods of the twentieth century after this, never was it a requirement for a respectable women in the way it had been during Victorian and Edwardian periods of fashion. Instead, as mentioned above, trends have tended towards the more freeing. Not only can women now show their legs, but they don't even have to wear stockings to do so. But this is not all. Women can show skin if they choose to, but nothing about the fashions today hold any one women to what she can and cannot wear. Style suggests but it does not dictate, and that is the legacy that is brought about by this integral period in American culture and fashion.

Above- (figure 1) - Stay, 1870, The
Museum at FIT.

Above- (figure 2)- German women,
Renaissance, *Bronwyn Cosgrave,
Costume & Fashion: From Ancient
Egypt to the Present Day.*

Left- (figure 3) - Early Victorian Style,
Gernsheim, Alison. *Victorian and
Edwardian Fashion: A Photographic
Survey.* New York, NY: Dover
Publications, Inc., 1963.

Left- (figure 4) - Levitt, Sarah. *Victorians Unbuttoned*. London, Uk: George Allen & Unwin (Publishers) Ltd. , 1986.

Right- (figure 5) - Edwardian Corset, http://www.trulyvictorian.net/tvxcart/ product.php?productid=110

Above - (figure 6) - The Gibson Girl,
Bowen, 1900-1910, 185.

Below- (figure 7) -The New Woman,
Ezra Bowen, *1910-1920*, vol. 2 of *This
Fabulous Century* (New York: Time-Life
Books, 1969), 40.

Left - (Figure 8) - Showing the ankles and neck, Peacock, *Fashion Since 1900*.

Right - (figure 9) - Loose belt, Peacock, *Fashion Since 1900*.

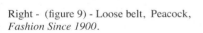

Left - (figure 10) - Military style
clothing, Bowen, *1910-1920*, 230.

Right - (figure 11) - WWI Style Trench
Coat, http:/
www.oldmagazinearticles.com/
article.php?Article_Summary=784

Left - (figure 12) - Slow decline of the prominent waistline. Bryde, *A Visual History of Costume*, 44.

Below - (figure 13) - Women in work clothes. Bowen, *1910-1920, 220*

Right - (figure 14) - Ways to conceal
alcohol during prohibition. Bowen,
1920-1930, 158.

Left - (figure 15) - Clothing advertisements, http://yesboleh.blogspot.com/2009/07/1928-summer-fashion-ads.html

Right - (figure 16) - Skirt lengths in the 1920's, Peacock, *Fashion Since 1900*, 70.

Left - (figure 17) - No waist and belted at the hip. Hershdorfer, *Coming into Fashion*.

Below - (figure 18) - the 'Bob' http://www.1920s-fashion-and-music.com/1920s-hairstyles.html

Left - (figure 18) - Cloche hat, Clark, *Hats*, 53.

Right - (figure 20) - 'Mary Jane's,' Swan, *Shoes, 64.*

Bibliography

Secondary Sources:

American Advertising: A brief History. last modified April 17, 2014.
http://historymatters.gmu.edu/mse/ads/amadv.html

American Cultural History- The Twentieth Century. 1910-1920. Last modified November, 2011. http://kclibrary.lonestar.edu/decade10.html.

Bruzzi, Stella, and Pamela Church Gibson, ed., *Fashion Cultures: Theories, Explorations and Analysis.* New York: Taylor & Francis Group, 2005.

Boucher, Francois. *20,000 Years of Fashion: The History of Costume and Personal Adornment.* New York: Harry N. Abrams, Inc.

Bowen, Ezra, ed., *1900-1910*, vol. 1 of *This Fabulous Century.* New York: Time Life Books, 1969.

Bowen, Ezra, ed., *1910-1920*, vol. 2 of *This Fabulous Century.* New York: Time Life Books, 1969.

Bowen, Ezra, ed., *1920-1930*, vol. 3 of *This Fabulous Century.* New York: Time Life Books, 1969.

Carter, Paul, *The Twenties in America.* New York: Thomas Y. Crowell Company, 1968.

Chambers, Clarke, quoted in Paul Carter, *The Twenties in America* (New York: Thomas Y. Crowell Company, 1968).

Clark, Fiona, *Hats: The Costume Accessories Series.* London: Anchor Brendon Ltd., 1982.

Crane, Diana, *Fashion and its Social Agendas: Class, Gender, and Identity in Clothing.* Chicago: The University of Chicago Press, 2000.

Dyhouse, Carol. *Glamour: Women, History, Feminism.* New York: Zed Books Ltd., 2012.

Ewing, Elizabeth. *History of Twentieth Century Fashion.* New York: Charles Scribner's Sons, 1974.

Fass, Paula S., *The Damned and the Beautiful: American Youth in the 1920's.* New York: Oxford University Press, 1977.

Gaines, Jane, and Charlotte Herzog. *Fabrications: Costume and the Female Body.* New
    York: Routlege, Chapman and Hall, Inc., 1990.

Gernsheim, Alison, *Victorian and Edwardian Fashion: A Photographic Survey.* New
    York: Dover Publications, Inc., 1963.

Greatest Achievements of the Twentieth Century. Household Appliance Timeline. Last
    modified 2014. http://www.greatachievements.org/?id=3768.

The Greenwich Village Society for Historic Preservation. Bohemia,1900-1929. Last
    modified 2014. http://www.gvshp.org/_gvshp/resources/history.htm

Gundle, Stephen. *Glamour: A History.* Oxford: Oxford University Press, 2008.

Herschdorfer, Nathalie, *Coming into Fashion: A Century of Photography at Conde Nast.*
    New York: Prestel Publishing, 2012.

Levitt, Sara *Victorians Unbuttoned.* London: George Allen & Unwin Ltd., 1986.

Lewenhaupt, Tony and Claes. *Crosscurents: Art, Fashion, Design. 1890-1989.* New
    York: Rizzoli International Publications, 1988.

Lurie, Alison. *The Language of Clothes.* New York: Random House Inc., 1981.

Museum of American Finance. Liberty Bond. Last modified 2014.
    http://www.moaf.org/exhibits/checks_balances/woodrow-wilson/liberty-bond.

Peacock, John. *20th Century Fashion: With 1100 Color Illustrations.* London: Thames
    and Hudson Ltd., 1993.

Peacock, John. *Fashion Since 1900: The Complete Sourcebook.* London: Thames and
    Hudson, 2007.

Riello, Giorgio and Peter McNeil. *The Fashion History Reader.* London: Routledge,
    2010.

Smith, Catherine, and Cynthia Greig. *Women in Pants: Manly Maidens, Cowgirls, and
    Other Renegades.* New York: Harry N. Abrams, Inc.

Swan, *Shoes: The Costume Accessories Series.* London: Anchor Brendon Ltd., 1982.

Topor, Lauren, "War and Fashion: Political Views and How Military Styles Influence
    Fashion" (2008). Master's Theses and Doctoral Dissertations. Paper 168.

Williams, James C., "Technology and Engineering in the American Experience."

http://www.cr.nps.gov/history/resedu/bb_williams.htm.

Weyl, Walter, *The New Democracy* (New York: The Micmillan Company, 1912).

Primary Sources:

President Coolidge, Calvin, quoted in Ezra Bowen, ed., *1920-1930,* vol. 1 of *This Fabulous Century* (New York: Time-Life Books, 1969), 96.

Dale, Samuel, *Chronicle* magazine, quoted in Ezra Bowen, *1910-1920,* vol. 2 of *This Fabulous Century.* New York: Time-Life Books, 1969, 228.

Hearst's magazine, 1917, quoted in Ezra Bowen, *1910-1920,* vol. 2 of *This Fabulous Century.* New York: Time-Life Books, 1969, 23.

Kastl, Norma B., *The Independent* magazine, quoted in Ezra Bowen, *1910-1920,* vol. 2 of *This Fabulous Century.* New York: Time-Life Books, 1969, 220.

La Guardia, Fiorrello H., quoted in Ezra Bowen, ed., *1920-1930,* vol. 1 of *This Fabulous Century.* New York: Time-Life Books, 1969, 154.

The Ladies Home Journal, quoted in Ezra Bowen, *1910-1920,* vol. 2 of *This Fabulous Century.* New York: Time-Life Books, 1969, 30.

The Literary Digest, 1918, quoted in Ezra Bowen, *1910-1920,* vol. 2 of *This Fabulous Century.* New York: Time-Life Books, 1969, 231.

Mencken, H.L., *Smart Set* magazine, quoted in Ezra Bowen, *1910-1920,* vol. 2 of *This Fabulous Century.* New York: Time-Life Books, 1969, 36.

The Outlook magazine, 1915, quoted in Ezra Bowen, *1910-1920,* vol. 2 of *This Fabulous Century.* New York: Time-Life Books, 1969, 46.

Robinson, Walter G.,*Vogue,* Jan 1913, pictured in Nathalie Herschdorfer, *Coming into Fashion: A Century of Photography at Conde Nast.* New York: Prestel Publishing, 2012, 27.

Roosevelt, Theodore, quoted in Ezra Bowen, *1910-1920,* vol. 2 of *This Fabulous Century.* New York: Time-Life Books, 1969., 208.

President Wilson, Woodrow, quoted in Ezra Bowen, *1910-1920,* vol. 2 of *This Fabulous Century.* New York: Time-Life Books, 1969, 208.

Images:

Primary-

Figure 1- Stay, 1870, The Museum at FIT

Figure 2- Painting of German Woman, Renaissance, pictured in Bronwyn Cosgrave,
     Costume & Fashion: From Ancient Egypt to the Present Day.

Figure 3- Early Victorian Style, pictured in Gernsheim, Alison. *Victorian and Edwardian
     Fashion: A Photographic Survey*. New York, NY: Dover Publications, Inc.,
     1963.

Figure 4- Victorian Corset, pictured in Levitt, Sarah. *Victorians Unbuttoned*. London, Uk:
     George Allen & Unwin (Publishers) Ltd., 1986.

Figure 6- The Gibson Girl, pictured in Bowen, Ezra, ed., *1900-1910*, vol. 1 of *This
     Fabulous Century*. New York: Time Life Books, 1969, 185.

Figure 7- The New Woman, pictured in Bowen, Ezra, ed., *1910-1920*, vol. 1 of *This
     Fabulous Century*. New York: Time Life Books, 1969, 40.

Figure 10- Military Jacket, pictured in Bowen, Ezra, ed., *1910-1920*, vol. 1 of *This
     Fabulous Century*. New York: Time Life Books, 1969, 230.

Figure 11- WW1 Tench Coat, pictured on
     http:/www.oldmagazinearticles.com/article.php?Article_Summary=784.

Figure 12- Lose of Waistline, pictured in Bryde, *A Visual History of Costume, 44*.

Figure 13- Women in Work Clothes, pictured in Bowen, Ezra, ed., *1910-1920*, vol. 1 of
     This Fabulous Century. New York: Time Life Books, 1969, 220.

Figure 14- Hiding Alcohol, pictured in Bowen, Ezra, ed., *1920-1930*, vol. 1 of *This
     Fabulous Century*. New York: Time Life Books, 1969, 158.

Figure 15- Clothing Advertisements, pictured on
     http://yesboleh.blogspot.com/2009/07/1928-summer-fashion-ads.html.
Figure 17- No Waist or Belted at Hip, *Vogue,* pictured in Herschdorfer, Nathalie, *Coming
     into Fashion: A Century of Photography at Conde Nast*. New York: Prestel
     Publishing, 2012.

Figure 18- The 'Bob,' pictured on
     http://www.1920s-fashion-and-music.com/1920s-hairstyles.html.

Figure 19- Cloche Hat, pictured in Clark, Fiona, *Hats: The Costume Accessories Series*.
     London: Anchor Brendon Ltd.,1982, 53.

Figure 20- 'Mary Jane's,' pictured in Swan, *Shoes: Hats: The Costume Accessories Series.* London: Anchor Brendon Ltd.,1982, 64.

Secondary-

Figure 5- Edwardian Corset, pictured on
http://www.trulyvictorian.net/tvxcart/product.php?productid=110

Figure 8- Showing Ankles and Neck, pictured in Peacock, John. *Fashion Since 1900: The Complete Sourcebook.* London: Thames and Hudson, 2007.

Figure 9- Loose Belt, Peacock, John. *Fashion Since 1900: The Complete Sourcebook.* London: Thames and Hudson, 2007.

Figure 16- Skirt Lengths Rise to Below Knee, pictured in Peacock, John. *Fashion Since 1900: The Complete Sourcebook.* London: Thames and Hudson, 2007.

I want morebooks!

Buy your books fast and straightforward online - at one of world's fastest growing online book stores! Environmentally sound due to Print-on-Demand technologies.

Buy your books online at
www.morebooks.shop

Kaufen Sie Ihre Bücher schnell und unkompliziert online – auf einer der am schnellsten wachsenden Buchhandelsplattformen weltweit! Dank Print-On-Demand umwelt- und ressourcenschonend produziert.

Bücher schneller online kaufen
www.morebooks.shop

KS OmniScriptum Publishing
Brivibas gatve 197
LV-1039 Riga, Latvia
Telefax: +371 686 204 55

info@omniscriptum.com
www.omniscriptum.com

OMNIScriptum

Printed in Great Britain
by Amazon

60902079R00037